T0379999

BASEBALL

Penguin Random House

THIS EDITION

Produced for DK by WonderLab Group LLC
Jennifer Emmett, Erica Green, Kate Hale, *Founders*

Editor Maya Myers; **Photography Editor** Kelley Miller; **Managing Editor** Rachel Houghton;
Designers Project Design Company; **Researcher** Michelle Harris; **Copy Editor** Lori Merritt;
Indexer Connie Binder; **Proofreader** Susan K. Hom; **Series Reading Specialist** Dr. Jennifer Albro

First American Edition, 2025
Published in the United States by DK Publishing, a division of Penguin Random House LLC
1745 Broadway, 20th Floor, New York, NY 10019

A catalog record for this book is available from the Library of Congress.
HC ISBN: 978-0-5939-6728-7
PB ISBN: 978-0-5939-6727-0

DK books are available at special discounts when purchased in bulk for sales promotions, premiums, fund-raising, or educational use.
For details, contact:
DK Publishing Special Markets, 1745 Broadway, 20th Floor, New York, NY 10019
SpecialSales@dk.com

Printed and bound in China
Super Readers Lexile® levels 620L to 790L
Lexile® is the registered trademark of MetaMetrics, Inc. Copyright © 2024 MetaMetrics, Inc. All rights reserved.

The publisher would like to thank the following for their kind permission to reproduce their images:
a=above; c=center; b=below; l=left; r=right; t=top; b/g=background
Dreamstime.com: Atoss1 7tr, 11br, Massimiliano Clari 8, Mexitographer 9br, Moodville 10, Mtsaride 38-39, Pictac 7tr (Bat), Rangizzz
32-33, Warren Rosenberg 9t, Angela Sickelsmith 16tr, Spectruminfo 28bc, 28br, Thelatin10 36-37; **Getty Images:** Archive Photos /
Underwood Archives 29tl, Al Bello 32br, Andrew D. Bernstein 43t, Bettmann 1, 21tr, 22b, 23cra, 24br, 26, 36crb, Blank Archives 25, Kevin
D. Liles / Atlanta Braves 27bl, Megan Briggs 35tr, Dylan Buell 44b, Jeff Carlick 40tr, Carnegie Museum of Art / Charles "Teenie" Harris
37tr, Jeff Dean 42bl, Stephen Dunn 27tr, Focus on Sport 30tr, 32cra, Matthew Grimes Jr. / Atlanta Braves 20t, Icon Sportswire 6, 22bl,
Kidwiler Collection 29cr, 39t, Kyodo News 41, Major League Baseball / Daniel Shirey 21b, Major League Baseball / MLB Photos 24cla,
Major League Baseball Platinum / National Baseball Hall of Fame Library 28cra, 28clb, 36cla, Ronald Martinez 40bl, Katelyn Mulcahy
20cra, 41b, Neil Leifer Collection / Neil Leifer 31tr, Photo File 38cra, 38bl, Photodisc / C Squared Studios 12br, Samurai Japan / Hector
Vivas 45, David Seelig 33tr, Sports Illustrated / Erick W. Rasco 44tr, Sports Illustrated / Greg Nelson 14-15, Sports Illustrated / Walter
Iooss Jr. 42cra, Scott Taetsch 34-35b, Transcendental Graphics 16br, 17, 18, 19, 37br, Universal History Archive / Universal Images
Group 23bl, Ron Vesely 33bl, Louis Van Oeyen / WRHS 23tl; **Getty Images / iStock:** Andipantz 7b, Apelletr 11t, DustyPixel 4-5,
E+ / Matt_Brown 30-31, E+ / Pixel_Pig 13, E+ / Quavondo 12t; **Shutterstock.com:** Elliott Cowand Jr 42-43, Joseph Sohm 28-29

Cover images: *Front:* **Dreamstime.com:** AJ Mears; **Getty Images:** Thearon W. Henderson bc, Michael Owens cr, Rich Schultz cl;
Back: **Dreamstime.com:** clb, Olga Novoseletska cra, Sonulkaster cla

www.dk.com

MIX
Paper | Supporting
responsible forestry
FSC™ C018179

This book was made with Forest
Stewardship Council™ certified
paper – one small step in DK's
commitment to a sustainable future.
Learn more at
www.dk.com/uk/information/sustainability

Publisher's note: This book uses terms for Black Americans as appropriate to modern and historical contexts.
Historical terms are defined in the glossary.

Level
3

BASEBALL

James Buckley Jr.

Contents

Play Ball!

Fans in the ballpark are on the edge of their seats. Millions more are watching at home. It's the final game of baseball's World Series. In a moment, one team will become the Major League Baseball (MLB) champion. The pitcher winds up. Here comes his pitch. Strike three! Game over!

Paul Skenes

Bat and Ball

A baseball is about nine inches (23 cm) around. It has a leather cover stitched over a tightly wound ball of yarn and rubber. Bats in the pros are made of wood. College, high school, and youth leagues usually play with aluminum bats.

Baseball has been around for nearly 200 years. It is most popular in the United States, Japan, and in some Caribbean countries. Fans are thrilled by how fast pitchers throw and how hard batters hit. And the drama of the World Series attracts millions of excited viewers each year.

Let's play ball!

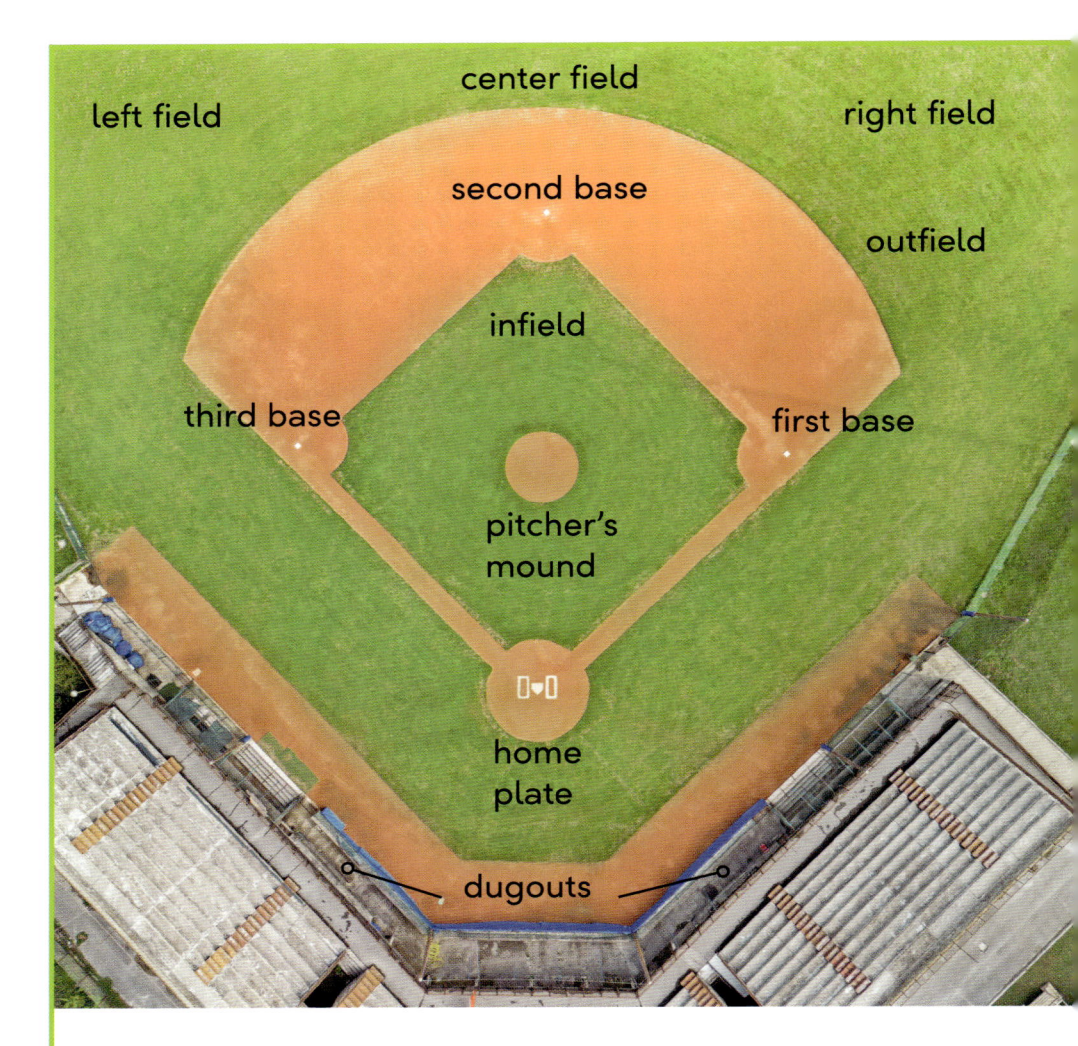

center field

left field

right field

second base

outfield

infield

third base

first base

pitcher's
mound

home
plate

dugouts

Baseball is played in a ballpark on a field called a diamond. The players from one team are on the field to play defense. Players from the other team take turns batting. Batters try to hit the ball into the field. Then, they run to the bases. When they get back to home plate, they score!

MLB is the top level of baseball. The league has 29 teams in the United States, plus one in Toronto, Canada. Lower pro leagues are called minor leagues. Baseball is also played in colleges and high schools. Youth leagues fill American parks every weekend in the spring.

Softball
While girls and women do play baseball, most play a variation of the game called softball. Softballs are larger—but not softer! Softball is a popular sport in high school and college.

On the Diamond

Baseball is played as a series of nine innings. The first team bats in the top of the inning, and the second bats in the bottom.

The team at bat keeps going until they get three outs. Batters can be out if they hit a ball in the air and a fielder catches it. Or if the ball they hit is caught and thrown to a base before they get there. If the pitcher throws three strikes, the batter is out by "strikeout."

The batter tries to hit the pitch into the field. After a hit, they run as far around the bases as they can. If they make it back to home plate, they score a run. The team with the most runs wins. If there's a tie, they play extra innings!

Types of Hits
Single Batter reaches first base
Double Batter reaches second base
Triple Batter reaches third base
Home Run Ball goes beyond the outfield wall; batter touches all four bases to score a run

umpire

batter

catcher

The most important battle in baseball is between the pitcher and the batter. The pitcher tries to throw the ball into an invisible box called the strike zone. This is the area above home plate and between the batter's chest and knees.

A pitch that passes through the zone is a strike. If a batter swings and misses at a pitch, that's a strike, too. The first two balls hit into foul ground outside the diamond are strikes as well. Three strikes and a batter is out.

umpire

A pitch outside the strike zone is called a ball. If a pitcher throws four pitches outside the zone, the hitter goes to first base. This is called a base on balls or a walk.

Pitchers throw the ball very fast to get it past hitters. They can also spin the ball to make it curve. Hitters have a split second to swing and try to hit the ball.

pitcher

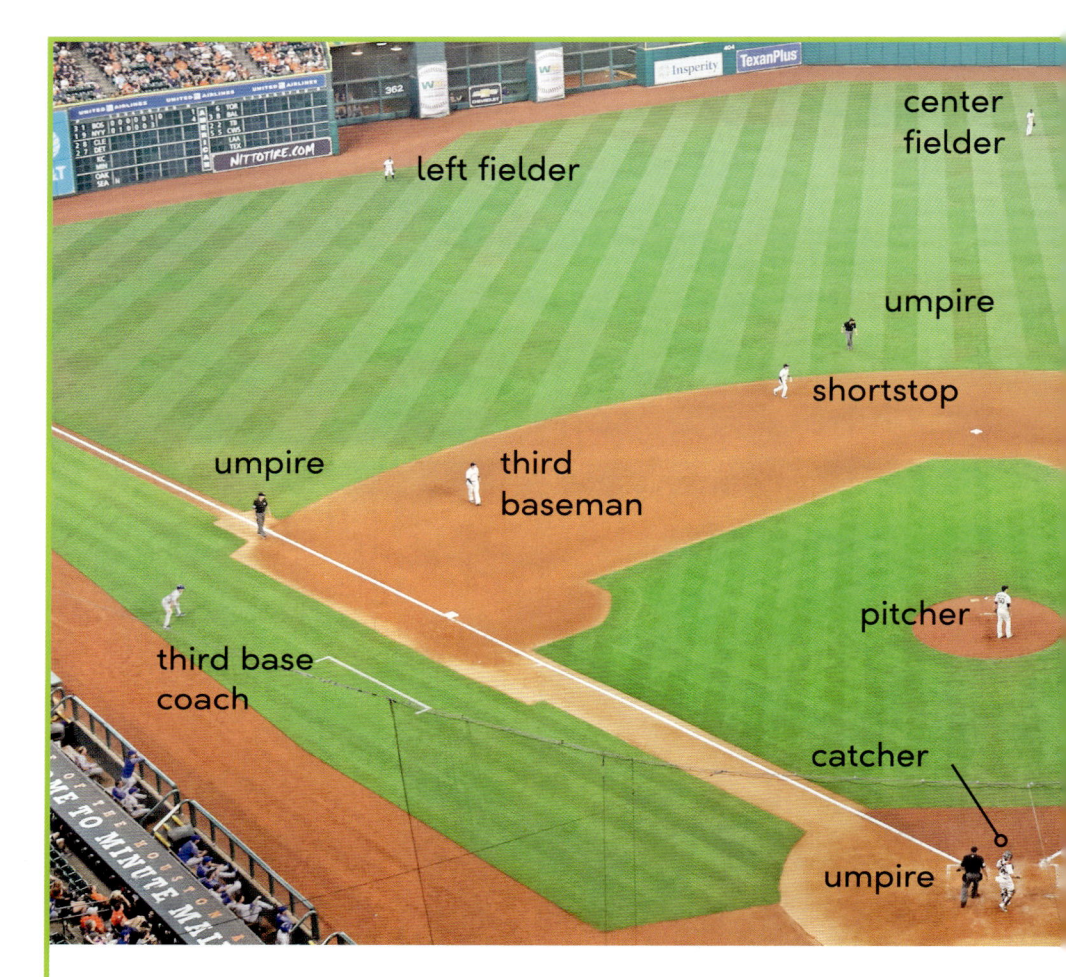

center fielder

left fielder

umpire

shortstop

umpire

third baseman

pitcher

third base coach

catcher

umpire

On defense in baseball, there are nine positions. There are three outfielders, four infielders, a catcher, and a pitcher. Each player covers part of the large field. They try to catch or stop balls the batters hit. The best fielders can make amazing leaping catches. They can dive to stop hard-hit balls.

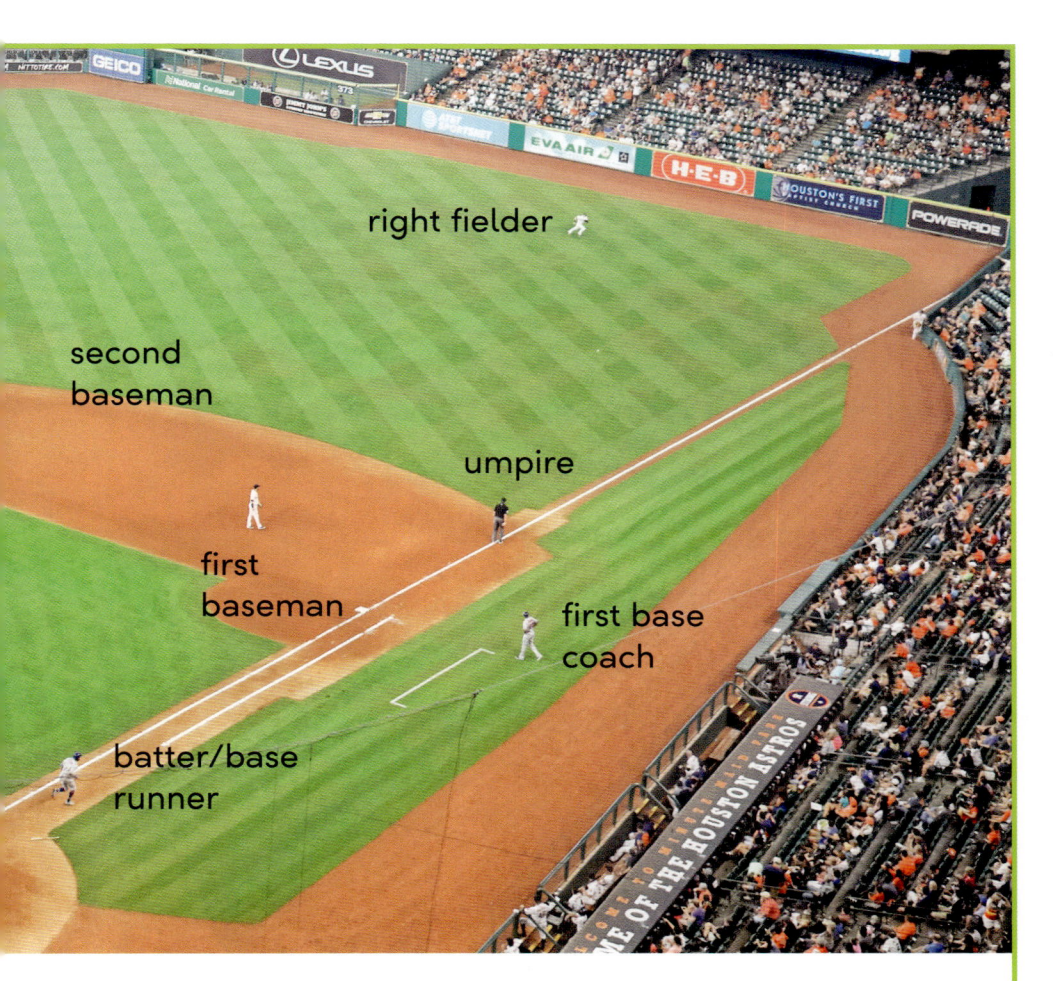

right fielder

second
baseman

umpire

first
baseman

first base
coach

batter/base
runner

After a batter reaches base, they become
a base runner. They try to move around the
bases as their teammates hit the ball. A
runner can also steal a base. That means
running as soon as the pitcher throws. If
the runner reaches the next base before
the defense can throw the ball there, they
steal it. Base stealing is exciting!

Baseball History

No one "invented" baseball. It evolved, or grew over time, from different bat-and-ball games. The first organized "base ball" clubs started in the Northeast US in the 1840s. Within a few years, hundreds of small clubs had formed.

At first, all the players were amateurs. They did not use fielding gloves. They pitched underhand or sidearm. It looked very different from today's style. But the sport kept changing. Players started using leather gloves. Pitchers threw overhand. Top players were paid.

Deacon White, catcher for the Detroit Wolverines, 1880s

The town baseball team in
Marlboro, Massachusetts, 1880

The first pro league was the National
Association of Professional Base Ball
Players, simply known as the NA. It began
in 1871. In 1876, it became the National
League (NL). The NL is still playing today
as part of MLB.

One big change since the early days of
the game is that pitchers don't hit anymore.
MLB now uses a designated hitter (DH) to
replace pitchers in the batting order.

In 1901, the American League (AL) was formed. The AL and NL came together to make today's MLB. The champions of the two leagues played the first World Series in 1903.

Baseball boomed in 1920. Babe Ruth became a star, hitting home runs for the New York Yankees. Even during World War II, baseball games were popular entertainment.

Game 2 of the 1916 World Series, Fenway Park, Boston, Massachusetts

Negro League star Josh Gibson, who holds the highest career batting average at .372

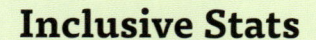

Inclusive Stats

Because of racist rules by AL and NL team owners, Black people were not allowed to play on MLB teams until 1947. Black players formed their own groups called Negro Leagues. Some of those players are now recognized as being among the greatest ever to play the game. In 2024, these players' career stats were officially included in MLB stats.

The biggest moment in baseball history came just after World War II. Since 1884, Black players had not been allowed in the Major Leagues. Racist team owners refused to sign them up. Finally, in 1947, Jackie Robinson joined the Brooklyn Dodgers. His inclusion was important to the growing civil rights movement in the United States.

Ronald Acuña Jr.

Shohei Ohtani

Baseball continued to grow steadily. MLB had 16 teams until the early 1960s. By 1998, there were 30.

The World Series is a hugely popular event around the world. Players from many countries play in MLB. By 2024, more than 25 percent of MLB's players were international, including superstars such as Ronald Acuña Jr. (Venezuela) and Shohei Ohtani (Japan). The World Baseball Classic began in 2006. It matches up national teams from around the world.

Women Take the Field

In 1943, many MLB players were away fighting in World War II. Philip Wrigley owned the NL's Chicago Cubs. He saw a chance to show fans a new type of baseball. He started the All-American Girls Professional Baseball League. Now women could play pro softball and baseball. The AAGPBL teams were mostly in the Midwest, including teams such as the Racine Belles (Wisconsin) and Rockford Peaches (Illinois). The league lasted until 1954.

Dorothy Harrell, 1948

At the 2023 World Baseball Classic

Highlight Reel

In nearly 200 years of baseball history, some highlights of the sport stand above the rest.

The first World Series was one. In 1903, the AL's Boston Americans (later called the Red Sox) played the NL's Pittsburgh Pirates. Boston won to capture the first MLB championship.

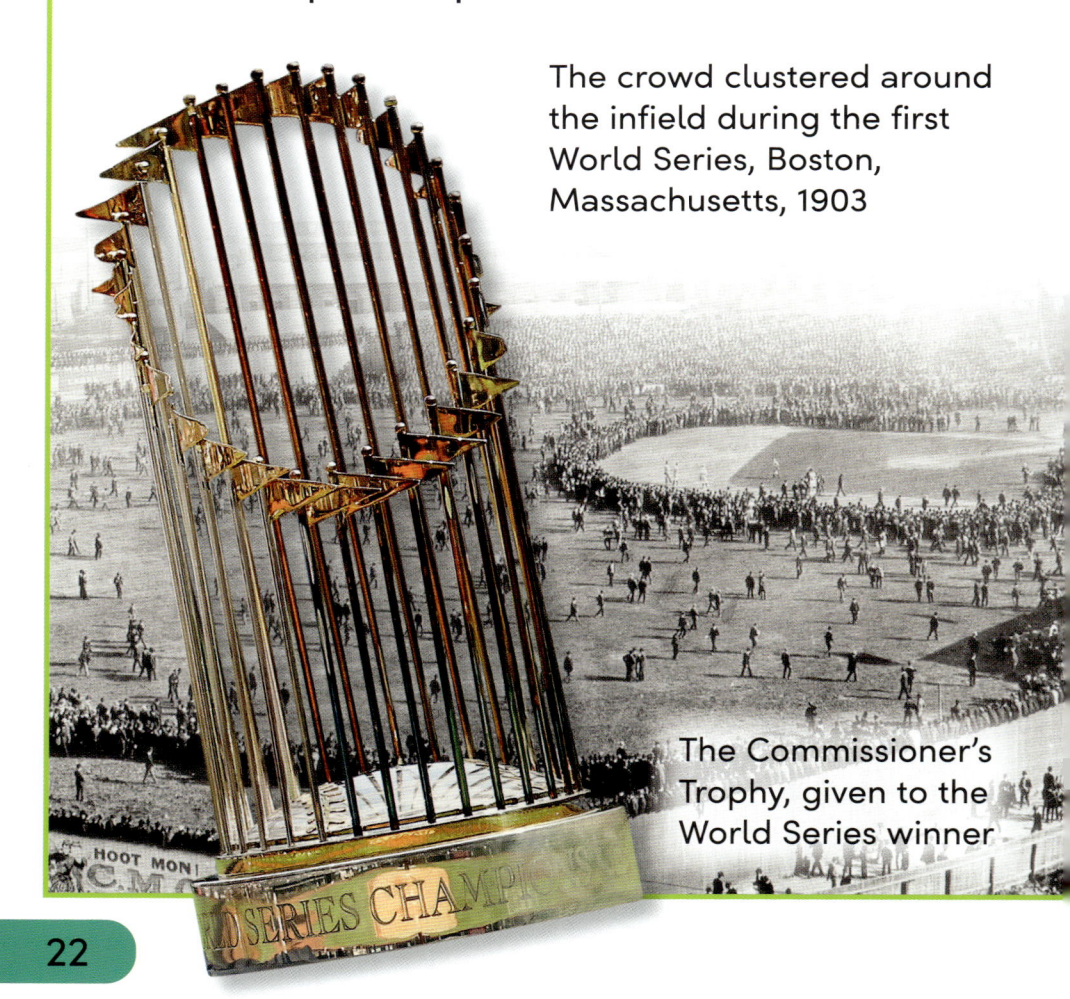

The crowd clustered around the infield during the first World Series, Boston, Massachusetts, 1903

The Commissioner's Trophy, given to the World Series winner

In 1927, Babe Ruth became the first player to hit 60 homers in a season. He thrilled fans around the league with his mammoth drives. He became a national sensation. No one would match his mark until 1961.

Babe Ruth

Ruth's Yankees teammate Lou Gehrig was almost as good a hitter. He had nine seasons with 140 or more RBI (runs batted in). He is considered the best first baseman ever.

Lou Gehrig

Jackie Robinson's arrival in 1947 was another baseball milestone. He led the Dodgers to the 1955 World Series. His tremendous speed energized the game. His courage inspired Americans.

Jackie Robinson

In 1958, the sport reached the West Coast. The Brooklyn Dodgers moved to Los Angeles. The New York Giants moved to San Francisco. Before that, the St. Louis Browns were the farthest western team.

In 1960, the Pirates' Bill Mazeroski hit a home run to win the World Series. His blow came in the bottom of the ninth inning. It was the ultimate "walk-off" hit (a hit that ends a game).

Bill Mazeroski

LA Dodgers pitcher Sandy Koufax created another memorable moment in 1965. He threw a perfect game. This means he did not allow a single batter to reach base. He is one of only 24 pitchers to have achieved that feat.

Sandy Koufax

The 1969
"Miracle" Mets

In 1969, the New York Mets surprised many
fans, including their own, by winning the
World Series. The "Miracle" Mets had only
been playing in the NL since 1962!

Some of baseball's biggest moments come when the biggest records are broken.

In 1974, Hank Aaron of the Atlanta Braves broke Ruth's career record by hitting his 715th home run. He retired with the record of 755 home runs. Barry Bonds of the San Francisco Giants broke Aaron's record in 2007.

Hank Aaron

In 1985, Cincinnati's Pete Rose got his 4,192nd hit. He broke a record held by Ty Cobb. No one has yet beaten Rose's career record of 4,256 hits.

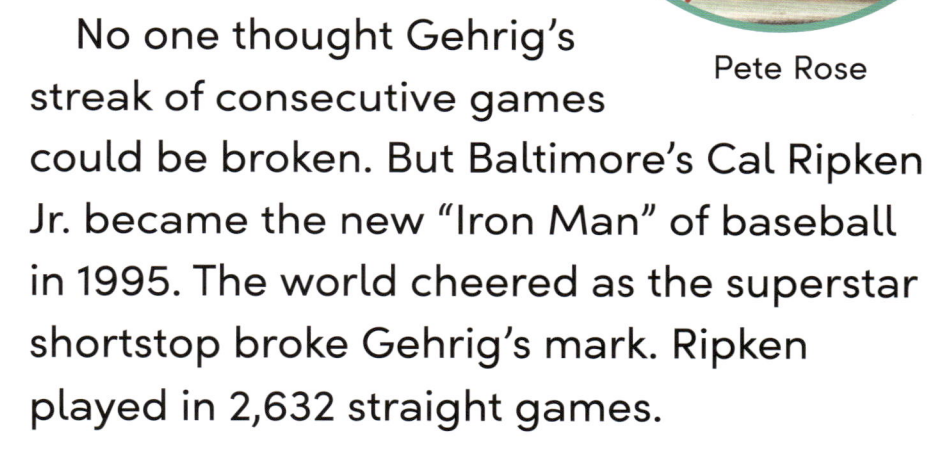

Pete Rose

No one thought Gehrig's streak of consecutive games could be broken. But Baltimore's Cal Ripken Jr. became the new "Iron Man" of baseball in 1995. The world cheered as the superstar shortstop broke Gehrig's mark. Ripken played in 2,632 straight games.

In 2023, Ronald Acuña Jr. became the first player to have 40 or more homers and 70 or more stolen bases in the same season. He had some of the best all-around skills ever!

Ronald Acuña Jr. stealing second base

Power Pitchers

Some of baseball history's first great pitchers are among the sport's legends.

Cy Young

Cy Young pitched for 22 seasons. He won an incredible 511 games. The award for each season's best pitcher is named for him.

Christy Mathewson

Christy Mathewson won 373 games. He was one of the best ever at preventing base runners.

Get a Grip

The way a pitcher holds the baseball affects how it moves on its way to the plate.

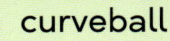
curveball

fastball

Walter Johnson

Walter Johnson threw so fast he was known as the "Big Train." He threw a ball faster than the fastest trains of the time!

Satchel Paige

Few pitchers were as entertaining or talented as Satchel Paige. Paige claimed to throw as many as a dozen different types of pitches. Most pitchers only use three or four! His teams often played exhibition games in the offseason, aiming for entertainment as much as wins. He sometimes told his fielders to sit down. Then he'd strike out the side (all three batters in an inning).

Sandy Koufax

Over six seasons in the early 1960s, Sandy Koufax won three Cy Young Awards. He threw four no-hitters and won five NL ERA titles. Koufax amazed hitters with his speed and incredible curveball.

Pitching Stats

Pitchers are judged by how many runs they allow and base runners they let reach base. Earned run average (ERA) shows how many runs they allow for every nine innings pitched. WHIP measures the total of walks and hits per inning pitched. In both cases, the lower the number, the better!

Bob Gibson

Bob Gibson was another 1960s star. He won seven World Series games while helping his Cardinals win two World Series. In one Series game, he struck out a record 17 batters. Gibson's 1.12 ERA in 1968 is one of the lowest of all time for a season.

A trio of Hall of Fame pitchers amazed fans and batters in the 1990s and early 2000s.

Randy Johnson

At six feet 10 inches (2.08 m), Randy Johnson was one of the tallest pitchers ever. He also was among the fastest. Johnson won five Cy Young Awards. He struck out more than 300 hitters in each of six different seasons.

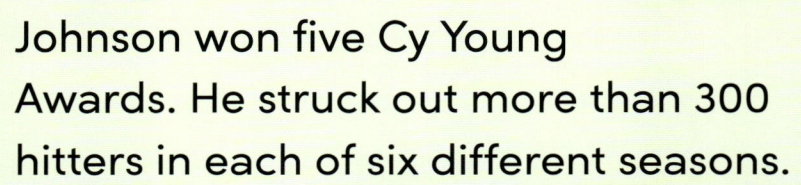

Closers

From about the 1980s onward, some pitchers took on the role of closer. A closer pitches very late in the game to "close out" a win. The best closer ever was Mariano Rivera of the Yankees. His 652 saves are the most ever, and he also saved 42 playoff games.

Mariano Rivera

Pedro Martinez

Pedro Martinez, won three Cy Youngs. He helped the Red Sox win the 2004 World Series. He had one of the game's best curveballs, too.

Greg Maddux

Greg Maddux was not the fastest pitcher. But he won four Cy Youngs by being very accurate with his pitches.

Hitting Heroes

Hitting a baseball is one of the hardest things in sports to do. To get a hit, the batter needs to hit the ball and make it to base safely. A player only needs to get a hit three out of 10 times to be considered a terrific hitter. That's called a .300 batting average. Because hitting is so difficult, a .300 career average is All-Star level.

Aaron
Judge

Batters have to make a split-second decision about whether to swing at a pitch. The ball can be moving more than 100 miles per hour (161 km/h).

Luis Arráez

Hitters' success is measured by their batting average and RBI totals. Fans watch how many homers batters hit. They also consider slugging average.

Some of the best all-around players played in the early years of baseball.

Honus Wagner

Honus Wagner played shortstop for the Pittsburgh Pirates for 21 seasons. He was a great hitter and a top base stealer.

Ty Cobb

Ty Cobb's .366 career average was the best ever until Negro League stats were added. Then, Josh Gibson's .372 put him at the front of the pack. Cobb was also a speedy runner; his 892 steals are the fourth-most ever.

Oscar Charleston

Oscar Charleston played 18 seasons in the Negro Leagues. He had a .363 career average. He led leagues in homers, RBI, steals, average, and slugging average. Later, Charleston became a championship manager.

Babe Ruth

The greatest hitter in baseball history was Babe Ruth. From 1914 to 1935, he hit 714 homers. He was also a star pitcher for several years. He had a high batting average and knocked in tons of runs. Ruth helped make baseball America's "National Pastime."

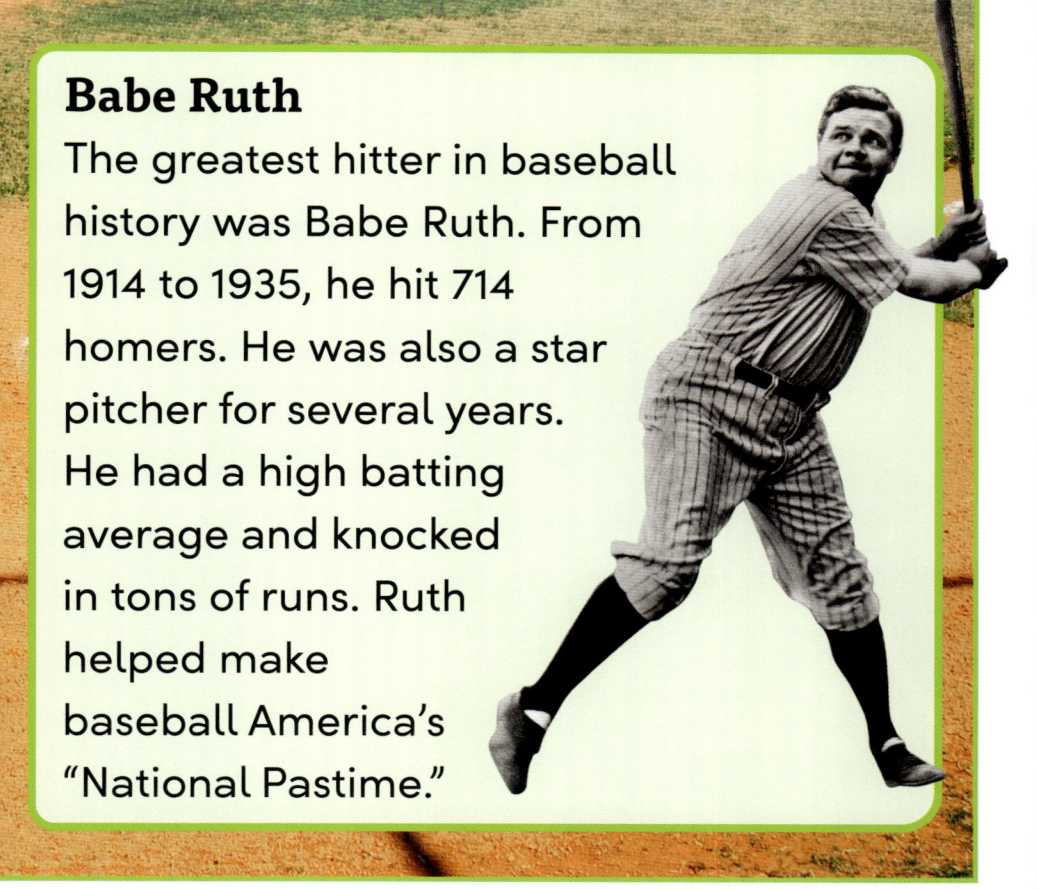

These incredible batters helped baseball boom in the years after World War II.

Ted Williams

Ted Williams grew up believing he would be "the best hitter who ever lived." Some fans think he was. He had a .344 career average. No one got on base more often than Williams. He won two Triple Crowns.

Mickey Mantle

Mickey Mantle combined speed, power, and fielding skill for the mighty Yankees of the 1950s and 1960s. He helped the "Bronx Bombers" win seven World Series.

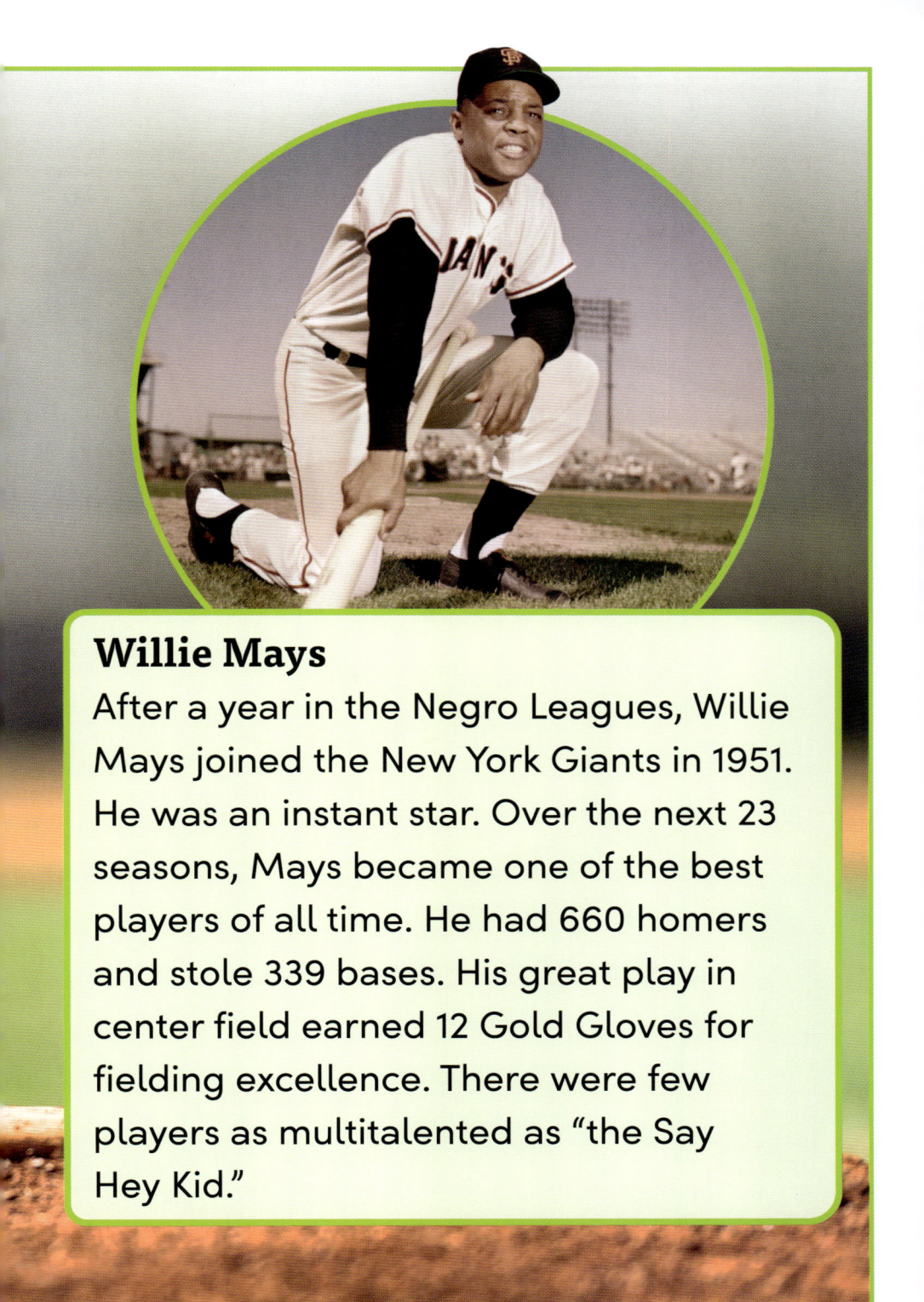

Willie Mays

After a year in the Negro Leagues, Willie Mays joined the New York Giants in 1951. He was an instant star. Over the next 23 seasons, Mays became one of the best players of all time. He had 660 homers and stole 339 bases. His great play in center field earned 12 Gold Gloves for fielding excellence. There were few players as multitalented as "the Say Hey Kid."

As the 2000s began, power hitters became baseball's biggest superstars. Barry Bonds set a single-season record with 73 home runs in 2001.

In recent years, the Dodgers' Mookie Betts is a fan favorite. He whacks mighty homers. He has played several positions, which is unusual in modern baseball. Bobby Witt Jr. of the Kansas City Royals is a rising star with both speed and power.

Mookie Betts

Shohei Ohtani

Shohei Ohtani is a star pitcher and hitter. He played with the Angels before he was traded to the Dodgers in 2024. No one else hits *and* pitches. Some say he might become the best all-around player of all time. In 2024, he became the first player ever with 50 homers and 50 steals in one season.

Super Speedsters

Speedy players who can steal bases help their teams win championships.

Lou Brock

In the 1960s, the Cardinals' Lou Brock broke Cobb's records. He had 118 steals in 1974 and 938 for his career. Brock carefully studied pitchers to learn when to run.

Elly De La Cruz

Today's best speedster is Cincinnati's Elly De La Cruz. He has electrified fans with his daring on the basepaths.

Rickey Henderson

Rickey Henderson is baseball's greatest base thief. He had six seasons with at least 80 steals each. His all-time best was 130 in 1982. He had 1,406 career steals—almost 500 more than Brock! Henderson also scored more runs than anyone in baseball history.

The Future of Baseball

Baseball keeps changing to get better. In 2023, MLB added a pitch clock. Now, pitchers have to throw to the batters before a timer runs out. This has sped games up. It also encourages more base-stealing, which fans love. Pitchers and catchers can now talk to each other through mini-radios in their hats. What's next? MLB is looking at using cameras and computers instead of umpires to call strikes and balls.

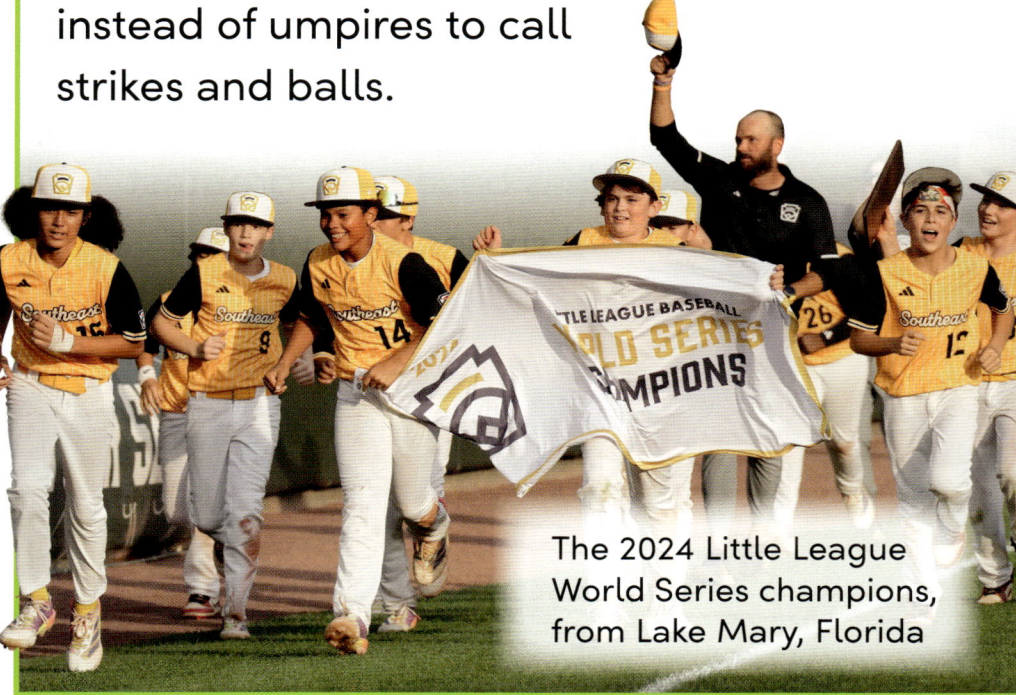

The 2024 Little League World Series champions, from Lake Mary, Florida

Ryan Otada during the WBSC World Cup U–15 World Championship Final, 2024

Baseball has spread across the globe. The game is very popular in Japan, where a pro league started in 1934. Mexico and several Caribbean countries have pro leagues. Little League Baseball has teams on six continents. And MLB has fans everywhere!

With such a rich history and a growing group of fans, baseball has a bright future!

Glossary

Amateur
A person who plays sports without being paid

Batting average
A measure of hitting skill, calculated by dividing hits by at-bats

Civil rights movement
A period in the mid-20th century when people fought for rights that promised equal opportunities and fair treatment for all people regardless of their race

Designated hitter
A player who replaces the pitcher in the batting lineup

Earned run
A stat that counts how many runs a pitcher allows the other team to score

Exhibitions
Games played for fun that do not count in league standings

Home run
A hit in baseball that leaves the field and allows a player to score

Inning
A period of play that includes three outs for each team

League
A group of teams organized to play a sport

Manager
The person in charge of a team

Negro
An outdated word for Black people, which can be considered offensive today; it can be used when talking about history, as with the Negro Leagues

Perfect game
A game in which the starting pitcher does not allow any hitters to reach base

Pro
Professional, or paid to do something as a job

Save
A stat for a pitcher who finishes a game for his team by allowing it to maintain a lead to the end

Slugging average
A statistic that measures the extra-base hits (doubles, singles, triples) batters make

Strike
A pitch that goes through the strike zone, or a pitch that a batter swings at and misses

Triple Crown
Leading the league in batting average, homers, and RBI in the same season

Walk-off
A hit that ends a game

Index

Quiz

Answer the questions to see what you have learned. Check your answers in the key below.

1. How many strikes does a pitcher need to throw to earn a strikeout?

2. What team did Jackie Robinson join in 1947?

3. Whose record did Hank Aaron break in 1974?

4. Who plays in the World Baseball Classic?

5. What is the shape of a baseball field?

1. Three 2. Brooklyn Dodgers 3. Babe Ruth 4. National teams
5. A diamond